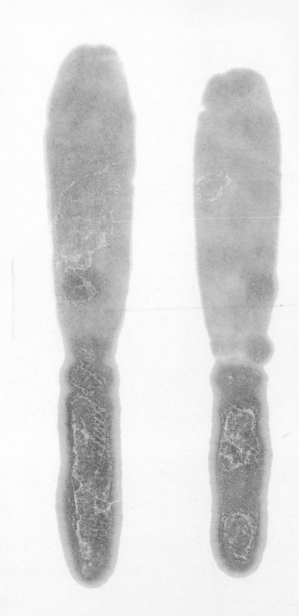

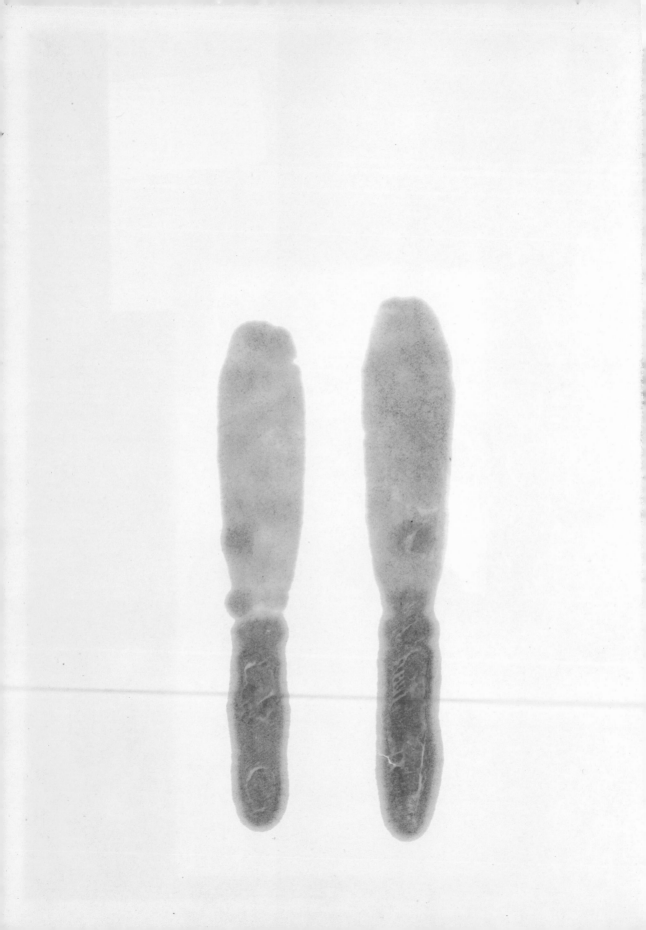

THE ROYAL BALLET

THE ROYAL BALLET

in performance at Covent Garden

by John Hart

FABER & FABER LIMITED
24 Russell Square London

First published in mcmlviii by
Faber and Faber Limited
24 Russell Square, London WC1
Printed in Great Britain
by the Shenval Press
London, Hertford and Harlow

Contents

Introduction

L ike many another photographer, I started as a disappointed artist, the paint and canvas kind; and as the ballet has been my life for twenty years, I began taking pictures of dancers in the company that I have been with so long—the Sadler's Wells Ballet, once the Vic-Wells Ballet, and now the Royal Ballet.

For *Ballet and Camera*, my first book, I photographed dancers in studios, at rehearsal and in dressing-rooms, on and off the stage; and in one sequence I tried to show the story of ballet in pictures as seen at a performance. This was Frederick Ashton's ballet, *Madame Chrysanthème*, and the pictures of it were the last ones taken for the book. Now I had found what I wanted to do—to show the ballet as we know it in performance at the Royal Opera House.

True enough, one can photograph dancers in a studio, and much of the work destined for magazine reproduction and for display in front of the house can best be done there; but, as with the matador in the bullring, a dancer gives a real *performance* only on the stage; and to photograph dancers anywhere else calls for a certain amount of posing and a false staging of a particular moment. This may be photography, but it is not ballet, so in order to take pictures of the ballet as presented on the stage I used my camera at actual performances, where the work of choreographers and artists may be seen in the atmosphere of the living theatre. This was the beginning of a heartbreaking business.

Naturally, the photographer cannot choose just any position in the auditorium, and these limitations control the 'angle' of the picture to be taken; this 'angle', in classical ballet, is most important. The ballerina may be wonderful, but perhaps the background is bad, with props, scenery and sometimes other dancers spoiling the whole shot. There is not enough light, the lens and the film are too slow, so you ruin the quality of the pictures which follow by trying faster films and developers. Then it's back to the dancers for another determined effort.

Many dancers are easy to photograph: the more co-ordinated they are in their movements, the more they tend to 'accent' or hold positions, the easier it is to get good pictures. Perhaps the more musical ones are the easiest of all, since one tends to press the shutter release on the music. Of course some dancers anticipate while others dance behind the music; some are apt to relax into a better position a fraction of a second after they have taken the pose; but others are perfect, and everything is quite simple. Naturally, classical ballet is the most difficult, for that which the photographer might consider a good picture is ruined for the dancer if the positions of head, arms, hands, body, legs and feet are not all perfect. Yet a ballerina in a perfect pose can look 'wrong' if the picture has been taken from a 'bad angle'.

So much for the difficulties. Now we are interested only in photographs, so let us look at the pictures and the ballets I have chosen from the repertoire of the Royal Ballet.

The Sleeping Beauty, *Giselle* and *Le Lac des Cygnes* head the list, three great classical ballets. Then we have Dame Ninette de Valois's *Job* and Frederick Ashton's *Cinderella*, and the last six ballets to be presented at the Royal Opera House—works by Cranko, Ashton, Macmillan and Rodrigues, who may be said to represent the modern British school as distinct from the school of Massine, Balanchine, Petit and Folkine, whose ballets, although an important part of our repertoire, are works primarily associated with other companies.

This is not a long list when one remembers that the Royal Ballet is about to present its fiftieth production at Covent Garden, but it is a distinguished and, I hope, an interesting selection. In choosing the photographs I have tried to introduce as many dancers as possible who have danced the roles, but above all I have aimed at illustrating the stories rather than at showing portraits of individual dancers.

May I offer my most grateful thanks to my wife, Margaret Dale, for writing the articles on the choreographers as well as greatly assisting with the remaining text, to William Wall for his invaluable help on the layout, and to Stanley Woodhouse and Frank Nicholls for printing the pictures. Moreover, I should like to dedicate this book to 'The Dancers', of whom it is literally true to say that 'without them a book of this kind would not be possible'.   JOHN HART

The Sleeping Beauty

Produced by Nicholas Sergeyev
after the choreography of Marius Petipa
Music by Piotr Ilich Tchaikovsky
Scenery and costumes designed by Oliver Messel

The Sleeping Beauty remains to this day one of the best-loved of all ballets, and as *La Belle au Bois Dormant* was first performed at the Maryinsky Theatre, St Petersburg, in 1890.

Marius Petipa based his scenario on Perrault's eternal fairy tale and his choreography included many gems, such as The Variations of the Six Fairies, The Bluebird Pas de Deux and the magnificent 'Rose Adagio'.

Tchaikovsky himself considered the score to be his best ballet music; it seems odd today that this magnificent and enchanting spectacle should have had a cool reception at first.

After the original dress rehearsal there were rumours that the ballet was unwieldy, that the music was muddled and difficult to dance to. Alexandre Benois in his *Reminiscences* recalls that he didn't even bother to get tickets for the first night. But Benois went to the second performance and says, 'I left the theatre in a rather hazy state, only feeling that I had heard and seen something that I was *going* to love.' These words would seem to reflect a general attitude, for after a while the ballet did become a popular success, and in fact led to a considerable revival of interest in ballet in St Petersburg.

Diaghilev's production, *The Sleeping Princess*, was first presented at the Alhambra Theatre, London, in 1921, with elaborate décor and costumes by Leon Bakst. It was a revised version of Petipa's ballet—there were several changes in the last act; Nijinska arranged a character dance for three men called 'Innocent Ivan and his Brothers' and several dances were borrowed from *Casse Noisette*; but in the main it was very similar to the *Belle*, having been reconstructed by Nicholas Sergeyev, who had made notes on the Maryinsky production. It was undoubtedly a landmark in the history of the ballet, and made a considerable impression on the English public.

Despite two occasions when the stage machinery did not function, the public gave it a wonderful reception on its first night, but it did not run for as long as had been hoped and Diaghilev suffered a great financial loss. Whereas *La Belle au Bois Dormant* grew to success after a doubtful start, *The Sleeping Princess* failed after a good beginning.

The next full-length production of *The Sleeping Princess* was given in February 1939 by the Vic-Wells Ballet, then a young and struggling organization. It was again staged by Nicholas Sergeyev, who had, as he told a member of the *corps de ballet* in his sparse English, begun his career by drawing Carabosse's chariot in the original production. 'When—first—Sleeping—Beauty—I—mouse!' he confided. A spare little man, he took most of the rehearsals himself, and he wasn't above swishing at the dancers' legs with his cane, in order to get the results he wanted.

The production was a modest one but it followed the original more faithfully than the Diaghilev version. The costumes and décor were by Nadia Benois and the leading roles were danced by Margot Fonteyn and Robert Helpmann. Acts I and III were performed at a Royal Command Performance in honour of the French President and Madame Lebrun at the Royal Opera House, Covent Garden, on March 22, 1939, and it remained in the repertoire throughout the war, though it was often presented in difficult circumstances and with depleted casts.

In 1946 the Sadler's Wells Ballet opened their first season at the Royal Opera House, Covent Garden, with a new production costing over £10,000. This time it was called *The Sleeping Beauty*. The costumes and décor, by Oliver Messel, had a delicate fairy-tale splendour. The cast was again headed by Margot Fonteyn and Robert Helpmann, Beryl Grey was the 'Fairy of the Lilac' and Pamela May and Alexis Rassine were the Bluebirds.

There were some alterations to the choreography; Frederick Ashton arranged a new 'Garland' Dance to the well-known waltz in Act I and also did the choreography for a *pas de trois*, 'Florestan and His Two Sisters', in Act III. Ninette de Valois arranged 'The Three Ivans' to music that had previously been a coda to the 'Aurora' Pas de Deux. Many of the names of the characters were changed and the Awakening Scene was placed so that it led straight into Act III.

In ten years it has been presented some three hundred times at the Opera House and a hundred and fifty times on tour. The role of Princess Aurora has been danced by Pamela May, Moira Shearer, Beryl Grey, Violetta Elvin, Nadia Nerina, Avril Navarre, Rosemary Lindsay, Rowena Jackson, Svetlana Beriosova, Elaine Fifield and as guest artist Alicia Markova.

There have been many memorable performances, but one which no dancer in the Sadler's Wells Ballet could forget took place in the Metropolitan Opera House, New York—it was the opening night of the company's first American season and it was indeed a triumph. After the performance, comments varied from, 'It's given a fairy-like quality to Broadway'—to 'Who would have dreamt that poor war-torn Britain could have produced anything like this?'

The Story

ACT I

Once upon a time there lived a good king, Florestan XXIV, and his Consort, to whom a daughter was born. She was named Aurora, because the dawn itself was never more beautiful. The christening was a magnificent festival, to which the fairies were invited to be present as godmothers. Six of them came and each of them in turn bestowed a gift upon the baby Princess. One promised that she would be the most beautiful creature in the world; another that she would have the wit of an angel; the next a marvellous grace in all her ways, and the others that she would dance to perfection, sing like a nightingale and play exquisitely on all the instruments of music. Suddenly a page burst upon the scene with the dreadful tidings that the wicked fairy, Carabosse, was approaching in dire anger at not having been invited to the christening. She arrived in a chariot drawn by mice and demanded to be shown the royal infant. In a terrible voice, she said: 'I promise that one day you shall pierce your finger with a spindle and on that day you shall surely die.' But the sixth of the fairies, the Lilac Fairy, had not yet bestowed her gift. She now stepped forward, and although she could not undo the harm her elder sister had done, she promised that, instead of dying, the princess would fall into a deep slumber that would last many, many years. One day a King's son would come and awaken her with a kiss.

ACT II

In sixteen years the little Princess Aurora had grown into a lovely maiden. There came to woo her four princes, and the King and Queen prepared festivities in their honour. The villagers were invited and the master of ceremonies saw that four of them had spindles. This was contrary to a law that had been made, making it a criminal offence to bring a spindle near the palace. The Queen intervened on their behalf as she did not wish the general rejoicing to be marred. But during the dance the young princess was approached by an old woman who showed her a spindle, a thing she had never seen in all her life. While examining it with curiosity, she pricked her finger. At her cry the dance ceased. The four princes rushed to her aid, but the old woman threw back her cloak and revealed the wicked fairy, who disappeared before they could reach the spot. The Lilac Fairy then proved that she had not forgotten her promise. She waved her wand and everybody fell into a deep slumber, not to be broken until the Princess should awaken. The good Fairy then commanded an impenetrable forest to grow round the palace and when all was safe she disappeared from view.

ACT III

Many years afterwards, the incomparable young prince Florimund (who was known to all as Prince Charming) happened to hunt on that side of the country where the tangled forest grew. He became separated from his companions. He was visited by the Lilac Fairy, who told him the story of the Sleeping Princess. He was slow to believe her until, with a wave of her wand, she showed him the Princess in a vision. But when he moved towards the maiden she vanished. Prince Charming then implored the Lilac Fairy to lead him to her, and out of compassion she invited him to step into her fairy boat.

ACT IV

At length the Lilac Fairy led Prince Charming into the Palace, which they found thickly covered with cobwebs. With some difficulty they found their way to the couch on which slept the beautiful Princess Aurora. Prince Charming tiptoed to her side, leant over her, and with one kiss broke the spell of the wicked fairy.

Never had there been such a wedding as that of the lovely Princess Aurora to Prince Charming. All Storyland was there. When all these people had paid their respects to the bride and bridegroom, the whole assembly joined in a great dance in their honour.

In an apotheosis the Fairy Godmother returned to bless the marriage.

'The Christening': the Court Ladies bow before King Florestan XXIV and his Queen (BRYAN ASHBRIDGE, PAMELA MAY)

The Queen inspects the 'list of guests'
while Cattalabutte (LESLIE EDWARDS),
the Master of Ceremonies,
assures the King
that everyone has been invited

The Fairy Godmothers, their Cavaliers and the Maids of Honour

The Fairy Godmothers and Maids of Honour bless the Infant Princess

The Maids of Honour

The Fairy Godmothers present their gifts

Suddenly, a crash of thunder interrupts the festivities

Out of the smoke comes Carabosse (RAY POWELL) in her chariot drawn by rats and mice

Carabosse pronounces the curse and laughs at the Queen's anguish

18

Carabosse is defeated as the Lilac Fairy (ROSEMARY LINDSAY) *says the Princess will not die but will sleep for a hundred years*

Princess Aurora's birthday festivities are momentarily interrupted as Cattalabutte shows the King and Queen the forbidden spindles

The Rose Adagio

Princess Aurora (NADIA NERINA) *dances with
the four Princes*
(DAVID BLAIR, DESMOND DOYLE,
RONALD HYND, GARY BURNE)

BERYL GREY

22

NADIA NERINA

Consternation as the beautiful Princess (BERYL GREY) *falls victim to the wicked curse*

The Countess (MARY DRAGE) *plays blind man's buff with Gallison* (FRANKLIN WHITE), *the Tutor,*
at Prince Florimund's hunting party

Prince Florimund (MICHAEL SOMES) *and his companions dance*

Together, Courtiers and Peasants dance a Farandole

Prince Florimund sees the vision of Princess Aurora

PHILIP CHATFIELD, BERYL GREY

ALEXIS RASSINE, NADIA NERINA

26   *With a kiss, Prince Charming breaks the spell* (NADIA NERINA, ALEXIS RASSINE)

Cattalabutte, the Master of Ceremonies, leads the guests in a Polonaise

The Blue Birds (ROWENA JACKSON, BRIAN SHAW)

The White Cat (DOREEN WELLS)

The Blue Bird (BRIAN SHAW)

28

The Blue Birds (ROWENA JACKSON, BRIAN SHAW)

*Princess Aurora and Prince
Florimund in the* Pas de Deux
(NADIA NERINA,
ALEXIS RASSINE)

The Three Ivans (RAY POWELL, KEITH MILLAND, BASIL THOMPSON)

The Apotheosis—The Lilac Fairy (BERYL GREY) *returns to bless the marriage of the Prince and Princess*
(MICHAEL SOMES, MARGOT FONTEYN)

32

MARGOT FONTEYN, MICHAEL SOMES

POSTSCRIPT

On December 12th, 1955, the Sadler's Wells Ballet production of *The Sleeping Beauty* was televised in colour from the New York studios of N.B.C. and in a coast-to-coast, nation-wide transmission was seen by some thirty million people.

These pictures, taken during the final dress rehearsal for this transmission, show Margot Fonteyn in perhaps her greatest role, as the Princess Aurora, with Michael Somes as Prince Florimund, in the Pas de Deux from Act III.

Dame Ninette de Valois

Ninette de Valois was born in Blessington, Ireland, in 1898. As a girl, she came to London and studied dancing, principally with Cecchetti, but also with Espinosa, Legat, Preobrazhenskaya and Zanfretta. If it is true that a dancer's 'pedigree' comes from her teachers, it is interesting to note these great names, for they are a fine representation of the French, Italian and Russian Schools.

At the age of sixteen she made her first appearance in pantomime at the Lyceum Theatre, London. In 1919 she danced in the opera season at Covent Garden, and in 1920 at the Shaftesbury Theatre. In 1923 she joined the Diaghilev Ballet and became a soloist. She was with the Company for two years, then returned to London where she opened her own school.

She joined the drama staff at the Old Vic in 1926, the year of the 'Great Strike'—Madame says she best remembers the important dates in her career by other events that happened, and adds, 'Although the "Ballet" began later, I've been with the firm now for over thirty years!'

It was in 1931 that Lilian Baylis asked her to provide a group of six dancers to perform in the operas at Sadler's Wells Theatre—a small but momentous event that proved to be the birth of the 'Royal Ballet'.

Today the Royal Ballet, numbering some ninety dancers, gives performances all the year round at the Royal Opera House, Covent Garden. In addition there is the Royal Ballet (formerly the Sadler's Wells *Theatre* Ballet), which was founded in 1946 with its headquarters at Sadler's Wells Theatre. This second company, which will eventually merge with the first, is at present actively engaged in taking ballet to the provincial cities of Great Britain. There is also a fully educational and partly residential school providing the dancers of the future.

During the twenty-six years of the Royal Ballet's history, Ninette de Valois has, with characteristic thoroughness, turned her hand to whatever job seemed to serve the most useful purpose. In the early days she was not only the Company's founder but also its teacher, ballerina, and choreographer. She has in fact created over thirty ballets. Recently, of course, her time has been fully occupied with day-to-day administration, planning and directing the policies of the whole organization. Two of her ballets are at present in the Theatre Ballet's repertoire—*The Haunted Ballroom* and *The Rake's Progress*—and the 'Rake' was recently mounted in Munich for the Bayerische Staatsoper. Two of her most important ballets, *Checkmate* and *Job*, are in the repertoire at Covent Garden.

When at work on a new ballet, de Valois comes to the rehearsal room with the ballet already prepared in great detail. She knows exactly what she wants, and if in doubt refers to some undecipherable notes on small pieces of paper, which she is apt to mislay. These occasions sometimes provide momentary amusement for the cast, for Madame's handwriting is not easy to read, and she has been known to require assistance in understanding her own notes! Generally a start is made by dividing the musical phrases into counts, then she painstakingly teaches the dancers the steps which she has previously worked out. De Valois allows the individual dancer very little licence in interpretation. She builds up the characters, usually by using highly stylized movement, and the dancer must be punctilious in observing detail, or the role will begin to get out of key. The advantage of her method is that finally the roles themselves are so tightly arranged, that the ballets withstand many changes of cast. For instance, in the past twenty-six years, the ballet *Job* has had several Satans, each consecutive 'personification of evil' being a different type of dancer to the one who preceded him; but it has always been the character of Satan that has come across the footlights so dramatically and clearly.

In this ballet de Valois used a plastic style of movement which suited to perfection the religious simplicity and power of William Blake's *Book of Job*. In other ballets, however, she shows a fondness for very precise movement and frequently the battle cry can be heard, 'Sharpen it up, girl!' When in good health, she is a positive demon at rehearsal; sitting on a plain hardwood chair, her body tensely charged, she forces the pace. She always remains quite oblivious of her spiralling stocking seams as she sits, with her legs crossed like a corkscrew, and one heel dug firmly into the floor, beating out the tempo for the dancers.

JOB BEING BLAKE'S VISION OF THE *BOOK OF JOB*

A Masque for Dancing by Geoffrey Keynes and Gwendolen Raverat
Music by Ralph Vaughan Williams
Choreography by Ninette de Valois
Scenery and costumes designed by John Piper
First produced: Cambridge Theatre, London, July 5th, 1931

SCENE I: Job is sitting in the sunset of material prosperity, with his wife, surrounded by his seven sons and three daughters. They all join in a pastoral dance. When they have dispersed, leaving Job and his wife alone, Satan enters unperceived. He appeals to Heaven, which opens, revealing the Godhead (Job's Spiritual Self) enthroned within. Job's Spiritual Self consents that his moral nature be tried in the furnace of temptation.

SCENE II: Satan, after a triumphal dance, usurps the throne.

SCENE III: Job's sons and daughters are feasting and dancing, when Satan appears and destroys them.

SCENE IV: Job's sleep is disturbed by Satan with terrifying visions of War, Pestilence and Famine.

SCENE V: Messengers come to Job with tidings of the destruction of all his possessions and the death of his sons and daughters. Satan introduces Job's Comforters, three wily hypocrites. Their dance at first simulates compassion, but this gradually changes to rebuke and anger. Job rebels: 'Let the day perish wherein I was born.' He invokes his vision of the Godhead, but the opening Heaven reveals Satan upon the throne.

SCENE VI: The young and beautiful Elihu enters, and by his dance shows Job his true relation to the Universe. Job realizes his sin of complacent materialism. The Heavens then open, revealing Job's Spiritual Self again enthroned as a glorified vision of the Godhead.

SCENE VII: Satan again appeals to Job's Godhead, claiming the victory, but is repelled and driven down by the Sons of the Morning. Job and his household worship, while the heavenly dance continues.

SCENE VIII: Job sits, a humbled man, in the sunrise of spiritual prosperity, surrounded by his family, upon whom he bestows his blessing.

ALEXANDER GRANT *as Satan*

The Vision of Job's Spiritual Self

Satan (ALEXANDER GRANT) *challenges the Godhead*

Satan's Triumphal Dance (ALEXANDER GRANT)

40   *Satan, War, Pestilence and Famine* (ALEXANDER GRANT, BRIAN SHAW, PETER CLEGG, KEITH MILLAND)

Job and his Wife (LESLIE EDWARDS, CATHERINE BOULTON) *with the Three Messengers*
(RONALD HYND, DESMOND DOYLE, PHILIP CHATFIELD)

Elihu (PIRMIN TRECU) *and The Three Comforters* (RAY POWELL, FRANKLIN WHITE, DOUGLAS STEUART)

Satan (ALEXANDER GRANT) *is thrust out of Heaven*

Job surrounded by his family

43

Frederick Ashton, CBE

Frederick Ashton was born in Guayaquil, Ecuador, South America, in 1906. His interest in ballet began at the age of fourteen, when he was taken to see Pavlova dance in Lima. This performance so inspired him that he determined to make his future somehow in the world of the ballet.

In 1924, Léonide Massine inserted an advertisement in the *Morning Post* which said that he was willing to accept pupils. Ashton answered the advertisement and as a result of so doing took his first dancing lesson from another great choreographer.

He confesses that at this time he was quite naïve about ballet and was under the impression, even when he saw the Diaghilev Company, that the cast made up their own dances as they went along. He also admits that his longing to dance was so great that one day he complained to Massine, 'These exercises you are giving me are all very well, but when am I going to dance?'!

In 1926, Ashton made his first venture into choreography with Marie Rambert, in the revue 'Riverside Nights'. They also performed in the ballet together; it was called 'A Tragedy of Fashion', and later, when Madame Rambert founded the Ballet Club at the Mercury Theatre, Ashton became the organization's principal choreographer. He recalls his optimism and excitement during the six-week run of the show—'I thought I was made—a leading dancer!'—and his disappointment at the end, when instead of receiving wonderful offers, he found himself out of a job.

The turning point of his career came in 1935, when he joined Ninette de Valois at Sadler's Wells Theatre and became principal choreographer of the Vic-Wells Ballet. The ballets which he created in these early years became the basis of the Company's repertoire. As one success followed another his versatility became evident and the demands made by his choreography helped to develop the talents of the young dancers.

With the exception of his war service, and one or two excursions abroad to create ballets for other companies, Ashton has remained with the Sadler's Wells Ballet and is now co-director with Ninette de Valois.

One of his greatest gifts is his ability to compose 'variations' and '*pas de deux*' around the talents of the particular dancers at his command. He is mainly interested in the ballerina but never neglects his soloists, and knows just how to exploit their individual styles and virtuosities to the full. He is such a wizard in this respect that one feels that, if he wished, he could build a variation around a dancer's technical faults and transform them *all* into virtues.

Once, when asked how his ideas came to him, Ashton replied that they were always there in his head in a vague way but that he could never say exactly when or how they came clear. 'It's rather like having a lot of kettles always on the stove,' he explained, 'every now and then, one of them just comes to the boil.'

Ashton's approach to choreography is instinctive rather than intellectual, and he seldom comes to the first rehearsal with any set ideas, though he always conveys to the dancers a particular mood or style that he feels to be essential to express the theme. At first everyone listens carefully to the music; sometimes dancers will suggest steps to him, and frequently he accepts these 'offers' as a starting point; though ultimately one finds that he adds to each step some very personal decoration or simplification. One great virtue of this method is that it gives each dancer a strong feeling that he also is contributing to the creation.

Ashton looks for choreographic inspiration in many things. Once during the rehearsals of *Scènes de Ballet* he produced a book of Euclid showing the dancers a geometric design which he wanted to use as a basis for a ground pattern. Having shown them the design, he let them work out the mechanics of the pattern, then with a sure touch completed the steps in an intricate rhythm, and added all the details that brought the passage to life.

He knows instinctively how to compose beautiful groups. He will approach the dancers without hesitation, raising an arm here, a leg there; he tells a girl to incline her head just so; he prods, he pokes, pushes and pulls bodies around, like a sculptor handling clay.

As a ballet nears completion, Ashton's nervous tension increases. He has been known to come into the rehearsal room despairing. 'I haven't got an idea in my head, but I dreamt last night that it ought to go like this.' Then he outlines something fantastic and improbable, and the dancers dutifully suggest ways and means of achieving the effect he is looking for.

As the first night approaches, no matter how well the ballet is going, he gets progressively moodier and more depressed; at final rehearsals he is apt to shout irritable instructions from the stalls: 'Why can't you keep in line, you silly girl!', 'What's the matter with you all!', relapsing into, 'Oh dear, it's all hideous!'

46

MARGOT FONTEYN, DBE, *as La Péri*

LA PÉRI POÈME DANSE

Music by Paul Dukas
Choreography by Frederick Ashton
Original scenery by Ivon Hitchens
Costumes by André Levasseur
First produced: Royal Opera House, London, February 15th, 1956

47

MICHAEL SOMES *as Iskender*

It came about that, at the end of the days of his youth, the Mages having observed that his star was paling, Iskender wandered through Iran, seeking the Flower of Immortality.

The sun dwelt thrice in its twelve abodes without his finding it, until he reached the extremities of the Earth.

And there, on the steps leading to the courtyards of Ormuzd, a Péri was stretched, sleeping in her robe of precious jewels. A star sparkled above her head, and in her hand shone the Flower.

And it was a Lotus like unto an emerald, undulating like the sea in the morning sun.

Iskender leaned noiselessly over the Sleeper and, without awaking her, took away the Flower.

Which suddenly became, between his fingers, like the mid-day sun over the forests of Ghilan.

But the Péri, opening her eyes, beat the palms of her hands one against the other and uttered a loud cry.

For no longer could she reascend towards the light of Ormuzd.

But Iskender, contemplating her, admired her features, which sur-
passed in delights even those of Gurdaferrid.

And he lusted after her in his heart.

In such a way that the Péri knew the King's thought.

For in Iskender's right hand, the Lotus turned purple, like the face of desire.

Thus, the servant of the Pure Ones knew that this Flower of Life was not intended for him.

And to regain it she darted forth, light as a bee.

While the Invincible Lord moved the Lotus away from her, torn between his thirst for immortality and the delectation of his eyes.

But the Péri danced the dance of Péris.
Drawing ever nearer, until her face touched the face of Iskender.
And at the end he gave her back the Flower without regret.
Then the Lotus seemed like snow and gold like the summit of Elbourz
in the evening sun.

Then the form of Péri appeared to melt into the light emanating from the calyx.

Iskender saw her disappear.

And realizing that this signified his approaching end.

He felt the shadow encircling him.

CINDERELLA

Music by Serge Prokofieff
Choreography by Frederick Ashton
Costumes and scenery by Jean-Denis Malclès
54 *First produced:* Royal Opera House, London, December 23rd, 1948

ACT I: THE KITCHEN

Cinderella lived with her father and two ugly sisters. The sisters were so selfish and bad-tempered that even their father was afraid of them.

One day they received an invitation to a court ball, and Cinderella looked wistfully on from the fireside as they prepared for the occasion.

While the ugly sisters excitedly imagined the forthcoming social occasion, at which each hoped to catch a husband, a mysterious beggar-woman appeared. The sisters drove her away, but Cinderella kind-heartedly gave her a crust of bread before she vanished.

Purveyors arrived, dressmakers, hairdressers, jewellers, and the sisters, each wanting the best, squabbled over everything. Of course it was plain to see that no amount of finery could have made either of them at all attractive, and at last when they were all dressed up they looked even more grotesque. But with a great hustle and bustle they set off for the ball, leaving poor Cinderella all alone.

Suddenly the mysterious beggar-woman reappeared, and throwing off her disguise said, 'Cinderella, I am your fairy godmother and I promise that you too shall go to the ball—for you are good and kind.'

She summoned the Stars and the Fairies of the Seasons, Spring, Summer, Autumn and Winter, whose attendants provided Cinderella with beautiful clothes. Then the Fairy Godmother transformed a pumpkin into a coach, but before Cinderella drove off in state she warned, 'You must leave the ball before the clock strikes twelve.'

ACT II: THE BALL AT THE PALACE

The ball was in progress when the Ugly Sisters arrived, and the jester danced in and out of the formal courtiers.

Shortly after the arrival of the Prince, mysterious music was heard, and Cinderella appeared, looking so beautiful that everyone thought she was a princess; and even the ugly sisters failed to recognize her.

The Prince was charmed by her beauty and offered her a gift of three oranges, the rarest fruit in his land. As they danced the time slipped by so quickly that Cinderella almost forgot the fairy's warning. In fact the clock was already striking when she rushed from the palace, losing a slipper on the way. As he picked up the slipper, the Prince realized that he had fallen in love with the beautiful stranger.

ACT III: AFTER THE BALL

A scullery maid once more, Cinderella listened as her ugly sisters described the events of the ball. Suddenly they were interrupted by a fanfare—the Prince was searching for his beloved, and had vowed to marry the girl whose foot fitted the slipper that he carried.

The ugly sisters tried desperately to squeeze a foot into it and, in trying to help them, Cinderella dropped the second slipper.

The Prince recognized his true love, and the Fairy Godmother appeared to bless the lovers, who lived happily ever after.

The Ugly Sisters try on the Slipper

The Prince (MICHAEL SOMES) *recognizes Cinderella* (MARGOT FONTEYN)

Cinderella and the Prince (NADIA NERINA, DESMOND DOYLE)

. . . and they live happily ever after

Birthday Offering

Music by Alexander Glazounow
Choreography by Frederick Ashton
Costumes by André Levasseur
First produced: Royal Opera House, London, May 5th, 1956

Dedicated to Dame Ninette de Valois, this ballet was written by Ashton to be presented at the Royal Opera House on the occasion of the twenty-fifth anniversary performance by the Sadler's Wells Ballet.

It is a divertissement created for the seven ballerinas and seven leading male dancers of the company, with an opening and adagio, a solo variation for each ballerina, and a mazurka for the seven men. This is followed by a *pas de deux* for the principal ballerina and her partner and the ballet ends with a final coda danced by the entire cast.

On the opening performance the ballet was danced by Margot Fonteyn, Beryl Grey, Violetta Elvin, Nadia Nerina, Rowena Jackson, Svetlana Beriosova, Elaine Fifield, Michael Somes, Brian Shaw, Alexander Grant, Philip Chatfield, David Blair, Bryan Ashbridge and Desmond Doyle.

MARGOT FONTEYN, MICHAEL SOMES

SVETLANA BERIOSOVA, ROWENA JACKSON, ELAINE FIFIELD, MARGOT FONTEYN, NADIA NERINA, VIOLETTA ELVIN, BERYL GREY, BRYAN ASHBRIDGE, DESMOND DOYLE, BRIAN SHAW, MICHAEL SOMES, ALEXANDER GRANT, DAVID BLAIR, PHILIP CHATFIELD

MARGOT FONTEYN, MICHAEL SOMES

John Cranko

John Cranko was born in Rustenburg, South Africa, in 1927. When he was quite young he showed an interest in books about the theatre and ballet. He had a small puppet theatre and spent much time making puppets. After fashioning his actors, he wrote plays for them, designed their costumes and manipulated them. His father says 'John was always very interested in making his puppets dance'.

Once, when he was about fourteen and on holiday in Cape Town, he had the opportunity to work with some professional puppeteers, and it was through them that he became really interested in ballet. They took him to the Cape Town University Ballet. He had never seen a performance of ballet before, and was so thrilled that he immediately decided to take dancing lessons himself.

He studied with Dulcie Howes and Cecily Robinson, and it was not very long before he was creating ballets for the Cape Town University Ballet and the Cape Town Ballet Club. As he grew up, Cranko plunged eagerly into the theatrical life of Cape Town, absorbing everything that interested him, but he continued to read all he could about ballet and the ballet companies abroad.

As soon as the war was over, he took the first boat to England, determined to join Sadler's Wells. Asked whether he thought at that time of becoming a dancer or a choreographer, he says, 'I just didn't think—all I knew was that I had to get to Sadler's Wells.'

He went to the school, and had only been there for about three weeks when one day a request came from the Sadler's Wells Theatre Ballet; they urgently needed a replacement, and it had to be a boy who could lift. Cranko was sent over to the theatre on trial, and he obviously managed the lifts without much trouble, because he stayed with the Company for the next three years.

At that time, the 'Theatre' Ballet was a newly-formed company of young artists, who danced in the operas, and gave one or two performances of ballet each week. It was largely due to Ursula Moreton, then the Company's resident director, that Cranko got his first opportunity to do choreography. Knowing how keen he was, she asked him to arrange a scene for the 'Angels' in the opera *Hansel and Gretel*. Later she suggested that he try a ballet for the Production Club of the Royal Academy of Dancing. This ballet was very successful—it was *Children's Corner* and was soon included in the repertoire of the Sadler's Wells Theatre Ballet. With this unpretentious but amusing ballet, Cranko made his mark, and there and then, London ballet-goers decided that he was a young man worth watching. Very soon, as he followed this first success with other works, it became obvious that his ideas flowed in many directions; for no two ballets were in quite the same vein. There was *Sea Change*, then *Beauty and the Beast*, *Pastorale*, then in complete contrast *Pineapple Poll*, a rich boisterous comedy which proved to be a great popular success.

Harlequin in April and *Reflections* marked a new phase, Cranko was, as he says, 'trying to make an image that means something—related to the meaning of life—which becomes more intensely real through being less realistic'. He goes on 'I want to get away from things that are only real in a photographic sense—I want my ballets to express something more than real—call it surreal if you like'.

In 1952, he created his first ballet for Sadler's Wells Ballet at the Royal Opera House. *Bonne-Bouche* was a lighthearted comedy peopled with caricatures, but in 1953, in *The Shadow*, he returned again to poetic unreal reality with a beautiful and simple theme. A young man is thwarted in his desire for romantic love by a dark shadow which comes between him and his beloved; when, finally, he takes courage, and confronts the Shadow, it crumbles into nothingness.

Cranko likes to invent his own themes, but they happen in a curious way; *The Lady and the Fool*, originally mounted at Sadler's Wells Theatre and later at Covent Garden, was built round many fragmentary ideas. Cranko says 'I wanted to do a ballet about someone who had everything, and who leaves it all for nothing! I also wanted to express in choreography an idea about two people who have something that they think is wonderful, but they both want it so much that they fight over it and destroy it'. This last idea became the Clown's 'Dance with the Rose'.

He often attempts to give extra depth to his characters in some purely theatrical way: for instance, the Lady who gives up everything is always masked to her wealthy admirers—no matter how many masks they remove there is always another underneath. It is as though she can only become her true self—without a false front for the world—when she falls in love with the ragged clown.

Prince of the Pagodas, a three-act ballet with music specially composed by Benjamin Britten, contains many theatrical devices. The Princess flies through the air to the Land of the Pagodas, where the Pagodas themselves, even if they do not dance, alternately beckon to her, and approach and retreat.

At work, Cranko is a great enthusiast. He works very quickly, for his ideas keep tumbling out, and often the dancers are hard put to it to keep up with him; for as soon as one passage is sketched out he is on to the next.

It is difficult to describe each individual choreographer's first approach to a new ballet, but probably the most amazing thing about John Cranko is the way he smilingly confronts his cast, calmly expecting the impossible.

BERYL GREY

THE LADY AND THE FOOL

Music by Guiseppe Verdi *arranged by* Charles Mackerras
Scenario and choreography by John Cranko
Scenery and costumes by Richard Beer
First produced: Sadler's Wells Theatre, February 25th, 1954

On her way to a ball given by Signor Midas, the Lady, La Capricciosa, finds two weary clowns, Moondog and Bootface, asleep on a bench. They dance for her and much to the disgust of her servants, she invites them to join her at the ball, where for the amusement of the guests, they present their 'act with a rose'.

The Prince of Arroganza, Capitano Adoncino and Signor Midas all admire the Lady and try to discover her true identity; but as each one removes her mask, there is always another underneath and finally, frustrated in their attempts to see her face, the three noble gentlemen leave her alone. She takes off the last mask herself and Moondog, the clown, catches a glimpse of her face as she runs from the ballroom.

Moondog loves La Capriciossa but feels she cannot love him in return because he has the face of a clown; yet she chooses him in preference to the three nobles who, shocked and angry, force the unfortunate couple to leave. The guests depart and Bootface is left alone, but the Lady and the Fool return and the three of them leave the ballroom together.

75

PHILIP CHATFIELD

The two husband hunters are stunned by the wealth of Signor Midas (GERD LARSEN, DAVID BLAIR, PAULINE CLAYDEN)

The Lady and the Clowns arrive at the Ball

The Lady called La Capricciosa is surrounded by her admirers, the Prince of Arroganza, Capitano Adoncino and Signor Midas (BERYL GREY, JOHN FIELD, DESMOND DOYLE, DAVID BLAIR)

La Commedia—Moondog and Bootface entertain the guests

Pas des Masques—*the Gentlemen try to unmask the Lady* (BERYL GREY, JOHN FIELD, DAVID BLAIR, DESMOND DOYLE)

Pas de Deux—
*the Lady and the Fool realize
they love each other*
80 (BERYL GREY, PHILIP CHATFIELD)

The admirers persist in their attentions

The Guests are shocked when she chooses Moondog, the clown

THE PRINCE OF THE PAGODAS

Music by Benjamin Britten
Choreography and scenario by John Cranko
Scenery by John Piper
Costumes by Desmond Heeley
First produced: Royal Opera House, London, January 1st, 1957

ACT I

The Emperor of the Middle Kingdom is in good humour as he drinks and dances with his courtiers, always led on by the Dwarf, a flattering servant of his favourite daughter, the Princess Belle Epine. After much gaiety the festivities are interrupted by the arrival of four Kings from the North, South, East and West, who have come to ask for the hand of Belle Epine, the heiress to the crown. She receives them; and after they have presented their gifts, she leads them with the Emperor and his courtiers out of the hall.

The Princess Belle Rose enters, attended by the Fool, her faithful servant. She is the much neglected younger daughter who has only beauty and simplicity for her dowry, but in a vision she sees the Prince of the Pagodas and for a moment she is lonely no longer.

The Kings return with Belle Epine, but on seeing the younger sister, the four suitors change their minds and each one asks the Emperor for the hand of Belle Rose. He refuses their requests and offers the crown to his favourite daughter. She accepts it immediately, but when the suitors reconsider their choice, she is furious and angrily rejects them.

In the midst of this great disturbance, four frogs arrive. They are messengers from the Prince of the Pagodas and have brought with them a magic casket. Belle Rose is the only one able to open this casket, from the depths of which comes a hand holding a white flower. She takes the flower and, escorted by the frogs, flies away from the Middle Kingdom.

ACT II

The Princess Belle Rose's strange voyage to the Kingdom of the Pagodas takes her past the Stars, Clouds and the Moon, the Fish and the Sea and the Rulers of the Fire, to the land of the Green Salamander, and the bewitched Prince of the Pagodas.

Hiding behind the pagodas, he shows her the wonders of his kingdom, and while her eyes are covered she is happily in love with the one she believes to be a handsome Prince; but the temptation to see him is too strong, and she tears off the mask, to find the Green Salamander at her feet. Frightened, she runs away.

SVETLANA BERIOSOVA

83

ACT III

Belle Rose returns to the Middle Kingdom to find the Court suffering under the tyranny of the new Empress, Belle Epine. Discovered by the Dwarf she is dragged before her sister, who orders the courtiers to hold her while she sends for their father. The wicked sister has kept the old Emperor locked in a cage, but she releases him for a moment, and the pathetic old man is overjoyed to see his long-lost younger daughter; but Belle Epine mocks him and forces him back into the cage.

At this moment, the Green Salamander appears, and with his magic releases the old Emperor and makes the wicked Empress and the Dwarf take his place.

In gratitude Belle Rose takes the rescuer in her arms; and loved by a princess at last, he is able to become his true self, the Prince of the Pagodas.

Free once more the Emperor consents to their marriage and gives his blessing; and on their return to the Kingdom of the Pagodas, there is a great celebration and they all live happily ever after.

DAVID BLAIR

Festivities at the Court of the Emperor (LESLIE EDWARDS)

The Princess Belle Epine, favourite daughter of the Emperor (JULIA FARRON) *and the four Kings* (GARY BURNE, PETER CLEGG, PHILIP CHATFIELD, DESMOND DOYLE)

The Princess Belle Rose, the much neglected daughter of the Emperor (SVETLANA BERIOSOVA)
and her faithful fool (PIRMIN TRECU)

*The Princess Belle Rose and the
Vision of the Prince of the Pagodas*
(SVETLANA BERIOSOVA, DAVID BLAIR)

The Dwarf (RAY POWELL), *Belle Epine* (JULIA FARRON), *the Emperor* (LESLIE EDWARDS), *Belle Rose* (SVETLANA BERIOSOVA), *the Fool* (PIRMIN TRECU), *the King of the North* (DESMOND DOYLE), *the King of the South* (GARY BURNE)

The Princess Belle Epine accepts the Crown of the Middle Kingdom

The Princess Belle Rose (SVETLANA BERIOSOVA) *and the magic casket*

The Moon (ANYA LINDEN) *rises above the Clouds*

. . . and sinks below the Clouds

Belle Rose and the Green Salamander who becomes the Prince of the Pagodas (SVETLANA BERIOSOVA, DAVID BLAIR)

Back at the Court with Belle Epine in power

Belle Rose returns from the Kingdom of the Pagodas

The pathetic old Emperor (LESLIE EDWARDS) *rejoices to see his long-lost daughter Belle Rose* (SVETLANA BERIOSOVA)

The Princess Belle Rose embraces the Green Salamander
(SVETLANA BERIOSOVA, DAVID BLAIR)

Released from his captivity, the old Emperor (LESLIE EDWARDS) *blesses Belle Rose and the Prince of the Pagodas* (SVETLANA BERIOSOVA, DAVID BLAIR)

Pas de Six (ANYA LINDEN, BRYAN ASHBRIDGE, MARYON LANE, GARY BURNE, MERLE PARK, DESMOND DOYLE)

MARYON LANE, DESMOND DOYLE

95

ANYA LINDEN, BRYAN ASHBRIDGE

The Prince and Princess of the Pagodas (DAVID BLAIR, SVETLANA BERIOSOVA)

SVETLANA BERIOSOVA

. . . and they live happily ever after

Kenneth Macmillan

Kenneth Macmillan was born in Dunfermline, Scotland, in 1929. Macmillan says that he has no idea how it was that he became interested in dancing, except that as a boy he loved books about the ballet, which he borrowed from the local library.

Ballet companies didn't visit Dunfermline, so he could only imagine what a performance must be like. 'But,' he says, 'I woke up one day when I was about fourteen, knowing quite clearly that I must dance.'

Afraid to tell his parents, in case they didn't approve, he went on his own to a local dancing school and took lessons for about nine months. During that time he continued to read all he could about the ballet and regularly bought *The Dancing Times*.

One day he saw an advertisement—and an opportunity! Sadler's Wells Ballet School were holding auditions for boys. He wrote a letter in his own schoolboy writing and signed it with his father's name. 'Dear Sir, My son is interested in joining the ballet! . . .'

He went to London, was given an audition, and was accepted for the Sadler's Wells School.

Nine months after that, in 1946, Macmillan was one of several talented students chosen to form the main body of the newly created 'Theatre Ballet' at Sadler's Wells.

Later he moved up to the 'first' Company at the Royal Opera House and in due course danced several soloist roles in the classical ballets. He had a good technique and was a very useful dancer, but gradually he became dissatisfied with his progress and asked de Valois to let him return to the 'second' Company at the Wells. There, he thought, he might find more opportunity to develop as an artist because the Company was smaller and they had a very varied repertoire.

About that time, there was at the Wells an enthusiastic group of dancers who were keen to try their hand at choreography. They organized a private Sunday performance which was to be a showcase for their efforts.

Macmillan says, 'I did think that I might try something—but I was told that it would be wiser to settle down as a dancer before attempting choreography, and it wasn't until the week before the show, when the programme was discovered to be too short, that I was asked to contribute a ballet.'

Somnambulism:—a study in nightmares to the music of Stan Kenton—caused something of a sensation. As the curtain fell on Macmillan's three restless sleepers, there was no doubt at all about the ballet's impact on the very professional audience present. In his first attempt he had revealed himself as a potential choreographer with not only a contemporary approach, a sense of humour and a highly individual style, but most important of all, real choreographic invention.

At first it was hard to say who was the most surprised at the discovery, the audience or the new choreographer himself; but he proved that it was no flash in the pan for, at a later 'Sunday Choreographers' Night', he produced *Laiderette*, a sensitive and mature work which Madame Rambert promptly requested for 'Ballet Rambert'. After this his talent simply could not be ignored, and Dame Ninette commissioned a work for the Sadler's Wells Theatre Ballet. The result was *Danses Concertantes* with music by Stravinsky and décor by an exciting new designer, Nicholas Georgiadis.

The greatest challenge of all comes to a young choreographer when he creates a ballet for the Royal Opera House, and Macmillan was not unaware of the difficulties involved when he undertook *Noctambules* for the 'first' Company in 1956. *Noctambules* was born of a desire to do a ballet about a hypnotist, and his first thought had been that it would be a comic ballet. But after the work was commissioned and he began to work out his theme in detail for the composer, Humphrey Searle, he decided that a serious approach would be more suitable. It became a ballet about hypnotism, and the effect of hypnosis on his characters: the Faded Beauty, the stunned, almost shell-shocked soldier who imagined he was a general; the pathetic Hypnotist's Assistant, and rich and poor people alike.

Watching Macmillan at work in the rehearsal room one is struck by the fact that though he works very quickly, it is all achieved quite quietly. His manner towards the dancers is persuasive, gentle and patient. He always knows his music well—long before he begins to think of steps, he spends hours at home 'soaking up the music' until he has the 'feel' of the whole ballet. At rehearsal he has a certain air of restrained eagerness and often he gets exactly what he wants right away; but if he is dissatisfied with any part of the choreography, he will change and change right up to the last minute if he thinks he can make improvements.

Noctambules

Music by Humphrey Searle
Choreography and scenario by Kenneth Macmillan
Scenery and costumes by Nicholas Georgiadis
First produced: Royal Opera House, London, March 1st, 1956

Rich and poor people are making their way into a variety theatre where a Hypnotist is about to give a performance. This is a failure, and his audience jeers at him angrily; by way of revenge, and in order to show his powers, he hypnotizes everyone. Strange things happen. The Rich Man and the Poor Girl see each other as if for the first time, and fall in love. The Soldier believes he is a general and the Faded Beauty, now surrounded by admirers, becomes beautiful; and under the spell of his own magic, the Hypnotist falls in love with her. Awakening from her trance, she tries to arouse the audience against him; but he carries her off before the crowd awaken to reality.

Finally, in a daze, they disperse, leaving the young lovers still absorbed in each other and the Hypnotist's pathetic assistant alone in her frenzy.

BRIAN SHAW

The Hypnotist (LESLIE EDWARDS)

*The Poor Girl Meets
the Soldier outside
the Hypnotist's Theatre*
(ANYA LINDEN, BRIAN SHAW)

Everyone is hypnotized—
the Faded Beauty (NADIA NERINA)
the Rich Man (DESMOND DOYLE)
the Poor Girl (ANYA LINDEN)
and the Soldier (BRIAN SHAW)

*The Soldier (*BRIAN SHAW*) imagines he is a general . . . and is shot*

*Imagining her looks have returned,
the Faded Beauty* (NADIA NERINA)
is surrounded by admirers

. . . but all ends in chaos and disillusion 105

Alfred Rodrigues

Alfred Rodrigues was born in Cape Town, South Africa, in 1920. As a boy he loved everything connected with the theatre, and always took part in school dramatics, but he did not know of the existence of ballet until 1937, when he was taken to see the René Blum Company. In his own words, 'That was when the madness started!' Andre Eglevesky in *Spectre de la Rose* made an overwhelming impression on him, and he immediately joined the Cape Town University Ballet, taking dancing lessons from Dulcie Howes.

Nowadays, Rodriques laughs at his youthful confidence, for with little more than a rudimentary knowledge of ballet technique, he immediately attempted choreography. His knowledge of the theatre and his natural enthusiasm must have carried him through, for, he says, many of his early efforts were given a performance by the University Ballet.

He had intended to come to England during the war, but joined the army instead, and was sent to Egypt and Italy; he didn't get to England until he was demobilized, but after that things developed quite swiftly; a chance visit to Vera Volkova's class led to an engagement as a dancer in a 'musical'; then, determined to aim high, he risked an audition for the Sadler's Wells Ballet, and admits that, while delighted, he was somewhat surprised that he was accepted.

Rodriques is exceptionally tall and has a good physique—very soon he was playing all the regal mime roles in the repertoire—the King in *Sleeping Beauty*, the Duke in *Giselle*, Von Rothbart in *Swan Lake*, and, also, gave memorable performances as the Russian Father in *La Boutique Fantasque* and as Job in de Valois' ballet of that name.

Later he became the Company's ballet master, and though he was always impatient to create ballets of his own, the arduous business of rehearsing other people's works gave him the opportunity of studying choreographic construction, and some useful experience in handling dancers.

His big chance came when Margot Fonteyn asked him to assist her in arranging a programme for a provincial concert tour, and to choreograph a small ballet.

The ballet was *Ile des Sirènes*, and later in the year, at de Valois' request, it was added to the second company's repertoire at Sadler's Wells Theatre. A few months later there followed *Blood Wedding*, based on the dramatic poem of Garcia Lorca—then *Café des Sports*, a comedy which featured a bicycle race in the authentic 'Tour de France' style.

Rodriques gave up his post as ballet master at the end of 1954 in order to concentrate on choreography. Since that time he has done a considerable amount of work for films, revues and television. He has also become extremely well known in Italy, where he has created several ballets for La Scala, Milan. Originally invited by Luchino Visconti to write a ballet for the opera *La Vestale* in 1955, he has returned every year, and to date has produced with his own choreography, Prokofieff's *Romeo and Juliet* and *Cinderella*, and Tchaikovsky's *Casse-Noisette*.

Rodrigues has an enormous sense of the theatre and invariably chooses a strong idea. He takes great pains to find the right composer and designer for each ballet, and has commissioned scores from Denis ApIvor and Anthony Hopkins, décors from Loudon Sainthill, Isobel Lambert, Norman Adams, Jack Taylor, Wakhevitch and James Bailey.

In the rehearsal room he works rather slowly and tries to perfect each scene as he goes along. The dancer gets the impression that he is tremendously interested in the way the roles are to be played, and the manner in which steps are to be performed. To press home a point, he will demonstrate a step, exaggerating sometimes quite flamboyantly the way he wants it done.

THE MIRACULOUS MANDARIN

Music by Bela Bartok
Scenario by Menyhert Lengyel
Choreography by Alfred Rodrigues
Scenario and costumes by Wakhevitch
First produced: Edinburgh Festival, August 27th, 1956

The scene of the ballet is a tawdry room in the busiest quarter of an unnamed metropolis. A street girl is forced by two hoodlums to lure likely prospects to the room, where they will be speedily divested of their money. Their first attempts bring in turn only a threadbare *roué* and a penniless youth, both of whom are brutally ejected. Formidable, but infinitely more promising of material reward, is a sinister-looking Chinese mandarin. The girl is frightened, but she seeks to attract him—timidly at first, then with unashamed sensuality. During all this the mandarin has remained outwardly impassive, only the burning glance of his eyes fixed upon the girl betraying the intensity of his desire. The reaction, when it does come, explodes in the form of the mandarin's relentless pursuit of the girl, whom he finally seizes: but the hoodlums break in and strip the mandarin of jewels and money. Determined now to kill him, they smother him with pillows; but he remains alive, trembling with passion, his eyes fixed immovably upon the girl. A knife is thrust into his body, but still his eyes fasten themselves upon the girl with unfulfilled longing. He is hung by the neck from a chandelier. The girl, with the instinct that is woman's, at last allows compassion to hold sway over her and embraces the mandarin with utmost tenderness. His unquenchable longing fulfilled at last, his wounds begin to bleed and merciful death comes to him as the curtain slowly falls.

ELAINE FIFIELD

A Street Girl, a Pimp and two Hoodlums look for likely prospects
(ELAINE FIFIELD, ALEXANDER GRANT, RAY POWELL, PIRMIN TRECU)

The first attempt brings only a threadbare roué (ELAINE FIFIELD, RONALD HYND)

The Chinese Mandarin (MICHAEL SOMES)

The Mandarin relentlessly pursues the girl
(MICHAEL SOMES, ELAINE FIFIELD,
ALEXANDER GRANT, RAY POWELL, PIRMIN TRECU)

The Hoodlums strip the Mandarin of his jewels and smother him

. . . but he remains alive

Then the Hoodlums attempt to hang the Mandarin

Moved to compassion the girl embraces the Mandarin

. . . a final look

. . . then mercifully he dies at last

Giselle

Music by Adolphe Adam
Scenario by Théophile Gautier *based on a theme of* Heinrich Heine
Produced by Nicholas Sergüeeff *after choreography by* Coralli
Scenery and costumes by James Bailey

Giselle was first presented at the Paris Opera in 1841, and is the oldest ballet still to be continuously performed by companies all over the world.

It is a romantic ballet and one which offers the ballerina a great role with an enormous range of expression. In fact it is often said that a ballerina regards *Giselle* in the same way an actor regards *Hamlet*, for it is a supreme test.

It is always interesting to discover how a ballet originated and Cyril Beaumont in his book *A Ballet Called Giselle* tells how Théophile Gautier was inspired by Heinrich Heine.

Just before the first night, the newspaper *La Presse* contained a notice of the forthcoming new ballet addressed as follows: 'My dear Heinrich Heine, when reviewing your fine book, *De L'Allemagne*, I came across a charming passage—one only has to open the book at random—the place where you speak of elves in white dresses, whose hems are always damp; of nixes who display their little satin feet on the ceiling of the nuptial chamber; of snow-coloured wilis who waltz pitilessly; and of those delicious apparitions you have encountered in the Harz mountains and on the banks of the Ilse, in a mist softened by German moonlight; and I involuntarily said to myself, "Wouldn't this make a pretty ballet?"'

Actually, Gautier was not the sole author of *Giselle*; he collaborated with Vernoy Saint-Georges who, it is generally believed, worked out the first act.

The ballet was an instant success, with Carlotta Grisi in the title role. The choreography has been credited to Jean Coralli, the *maître de ballet* of the Opera, though there is some evidence to suppose that Jules Perrot, Carlotta's husband and teacher, was responsible for her solos and some of the scenes in which she appeared.

The first time *Giselle* was produced in London was in 1842 at Her Majesty's Theatre, again with Grisi in the leading role.

Another important London production was one presented by the Diaghilev Company in 1911 at the Royal Opera House, Covent Garden, with Karsavina and Nijinsky. Anna Pavlova danced the role, supported by her own company, in London in 1913.

In St Petersburg the first production was in 1842 and the ballet has remained in the repertoire of the State Theatres in Russia ever since.

It is interesting to note that during the recent visit of the Moscow Bolshoi Ballet to London, *Giselle* was received with almost more enthusiasm than any other ballet, and the choreography was only very slightly different to the version to which the London public are accustomed.

Nicholas Sergeyev revived the ballet for the Vic-Wells Ballet in 1934, when the leading role was danced by Alicia Markova. Since then there have been three revivals by the Sadler's Wells Ballet, in 1935, 1946 and 1951, and the role has been danced by Alicia Markova, Margot Fonteyn, June Brae, Beryl Grey, Moira Shearer, Violetta Elvin, Pauline Clayden, Anne Heaton, Nadia Nerina and Svetlana Beriosova.

The Story

ACT I: GISELLE'S COTTAGE IN THE WOOD

Giselle, peasant maiden, is loved by Count Albrecht, whom she knows as Loys. A meeting between them is interrupted by Hilarion, a huntsman, whose love Giselle has rejected. Hilarion knows Loys' identity, having found a crested sword in the latter's dwelling. At the grape harvest celebration the Duke of Courland appears, accompanied by his daughter, the Princess, to whom Albrecht is betrothed. Giselle's sweet simplicity charms the Princess. Later, when Giselle is dancing for the village maidens, Hilarion returns, and chooses this moment for his revenge. Displaying the sword to Giselle, he unmasks the feigned Loys, who admits his deception. Realizing her love is bestowed on one who can never be hers, Giselle becomes distracted, and in her madness, going through the steps of her last dance with her beloved Loys, kills herself with his sword.

ACT II: GISELLE'S TOMB IN THE FOREST

The Wilis are dancing—young women who, according to Slavonic tradition, perishing on the eve of marriage, cannot rest in their tombs. Their Queen initiates Giselle. Coming to visit her tomb, the mourning Albrecht encounters her. The Wilis drive Hilarion into the lake, and Albrecht is commanded to dance until he drops dead. With Giselle he dances without respite, but, sustained by her love, he survives until dawn, when the power of the Wilis ceases. Then, seeing Giselle about to return to her tomb, the exhausted Albrecht bars the way and gently lays her on a bank, where flowers arise and cover her.

VIOLETTA ELVIN

Giselle and the Count Albrecht whom she knows as Loys, a peasant

VIOLETTA ELVIN, JOHN FIELD

NADIA NERINA, ALEXIS RASSINE

They dance at the grape-harvest celebration (VIOLETTA ELVIN, JOHN FIELD)

NADIA NERINA, ALEXIS RASSINE

Giselle's Mother (ELISABETH KENNEDY) *interrupts the celebration because she believes her daughter will die if she dances* (NADIA NERINA, ALEXIS RASSINE)

VIOLETTA ELVIN, JOHN FIELD, ELISABETH KENNEDY

The Duke of Courland and his daughter Bathilda arrive with a hunting party (BRYAN ASHBRIDGE, JULIA FARRON, VIOLETTA ELVIN)

123

The Princess Bathilda, charmed with Giselle's grace, gives her a necklace

Hilarion, determined to unmask Loys, the disguised nobleman, recalls the Duke's hunting party (VIOLETTA ELVIN, LESLIE

124   EDWARDS)

Giselle cannot believe that the man she loves is betrothed to the Princess
(VIOLETTA ELVIN, JULIA FARRON, JOHN FIELD)

Giselle, in her madness, recalls her dance with Loys
(VIOLETTA ELVIN, JOHN FIELD)

She seizes his sword (VIOLETTA ELVIN)

Distraught, Giselle runs to her mother (NADIA NERINA, ELISABETH KENNEDY)

Giselle throws a sad despairing glance at Loys as her eyes close for ever

The Count Albrecht is crazed with love and despair (PHILIP CHATFIELD, SVETLANA BERIOSOVA)

Led by their Queen (ANYA LINDEN), *the Wilis are dancing*

Coming to visit her tomb, Albrecht encounters Giselle, now a Wili (SVETLANA BERIOSOVA, PHILIP CHATFIELD)

The Wilis surround Hilarion and the Queen sends him to his death (LESLIE EDWARDS, ROWENA JACKSON)

Giselle comforts the enchanted Albrecht as the Wilis, seeing the approach of dawn, prepare to return to their tombs (SVETLANA
BERIOSOVA, PHILIP CHATFIELD)

LE LAC DES CYGNES

Music by Piotr Ilich Tchaikovsky
Choreography by Marius Petipa and Lev Ivanov
Produced by Nicholas Sergeyev
Present production revised by Ninette de Valois
Choreography for the Pas de Six in Act I and
the Neapolitan Dance in Act III by Frederick Ashton
Scenery and costumes by Leslie Hurry

When this ballet was first produced at the Bolshoi Theatre, Moscow, in 1877 with choreography by Julius Reisinger, it was a failure and was soon taken out of the repertoire. The four-act version with which we are familiar in this country is based on a production given at the Maryinsky Theatre, St Petersburg, in 1895, two years after Tchaikovsky's death, with choreography by Marius Petipa and Lev Ivanov.

It is sad to think that Tchaikovsky who, after all, wrote some of the most beautiful ballet music in the world, died before any of his ballets achieved success.

Diaghilev didn't include the four-act version of *Le Lac des Cygnes* in his repertoire—he believed it to be too long and old-fashioned.

The first revival by the Vic-Wells Ballet was staged by Nicholas Sergeyev and presented at Sadler's Wells Theatre in November 1934 with Alicia Markova and Robert Helpmann in the principal roles.

The present production, which was revised by Dame Ninette de Valois, was first given at the Royal Opera House, Covent Garden, in December 1952 in the presence of HM the Queen Mother and HRH Princess Margaret. The décor and costumes by Leslie Hurry were his third set of designs for this ballet; they were a little more conventional than his earlier designs which had been used during the war, and were considered to be very successful.

Frederick Ashton arranged two new dances for this production: a *pas de six* was placed at the beginning of Act I, and a very bright 'Neapolitan Dance' was included in the divertissement in Act III.

The exacting dual role of Odette/Odile has been danced by many of the ballerinas of the Royal Ballet—Margot Fonteyn, Beryl Grey, Nadia Nerina, Rowena Jackson, Svetlana Beriosova and Elaine Fifield.

ROWENA JACKSON

The Story

ACT I: THE GARDEN OF THE CASTLE

It is Prince Siegfried's twenty-first birthday. His friend Benno and his tutor Wolfgang await the Prince in the castle grounds where villagers have been assembled to provide dances in honour of the occasion. The Prince arrives and in the midst of the ensuing festivities the Princess Mother pays an unexpected visit. She does not approve of the Prince's companions and expresses her displeasure. Before her departure she reminds him that, having now come of age, he must choose a bride at a Ball she has commanded to be held on the morrow.

As the day draws to a close, the peasants take their leave. The Prince's friends see a flock of swans flying overhead. His friends decide to hunt them and Benno persuades the Prince to join in the chase. They leave the castle grounds together.

ACT II: THE LAKESIDE BY MOONLIGHT

The huntsmen sight the swans and inform the Prince, but he prefers to remain alone with his thoughts. Suddenly, he sees a swan approaching, but on reaching the bank the swan is transformed into a beautiful maiden. She tells him that she is the Princess Odette and that she and her companions are victims of an evil enchanter who has bewitched them. Only at night are they permitted to return to human form, and even then their master watches over them in the guise of an owl. Odette's enchantment can only be broken if someone falls in love with her who has never before plighted his troth. The enchanter appears and Odette begs him not to harm the Prince. Siegfried attempts to shoot the magician but Odette stays his hand.

Swan-maidens fill the glade and Benno returns and becomes encircled by them. He calls to the other huntsman who, owing to the mist, mistake the frightened maidens for swans and prepare to shoot them.

The Prince returns in time to prevent the shooting and Odette asks for his protection. The swan-maidens dance and the Prince enters with Benno and searches among them for Odette. Suddenly she appears again in their midst and Odette and the Prince express their love for each other. Siegfried tries to restrain Odette from leaving him, but she and her companions must, with the approach of dawn, re-enter the lake and resume their guise as swans.

The Prince is left to mourn her departure, and with his companions gazes sadly after the flight of swans traversing the sky.

ACT III: THE BALLROOM OF THE CASTLE

The Master of Ceremonies and ladies of the court await the Princess Mother, the Prince and their guests. All assemble and the Prince is asked to dance with six young girls. The Princess Mother desires him to choose one for his bride, but none pleases him, for his thoughts are full of Odette.

Suddenly two uninvited guests are announced. They are the magician now in human form and calling himself the Baron von Rothbart, and his daughter Odile, who enter the ballroom. The Prince stands transfixed; he sees the unknown visitor's striking resemblance to Odette and is certain that she is his Swan Princess.

The Ball continues and the Prince dances with Odile. During the dance a vision of Odette appears beseeching Siegfried to remember her, but he fails to observe it. Infatuated, he asks for Odile's hand in marriage. Von Rothbart makes him swear that Odile is his chosen love. Having sworn, at that moment he sees the vision of Odette. It is too late; he has pledged his word to another. The Swan Princess must remain in the enchanter's power. Rothbart and Odile vanish and the Court is thrown into confusion. In despair the Prince rushes out, in search of his lost love.

ACT IV: THE LAKESIDE

The swan-maidens anxiously await Odette. She returns distraught, for life now holds no joy for her. She wishes to drown herself in the waters of the lake while she is in her human form. The glade is overcast by a storm and as it clears the distracted Siegfried arrives. He seeks Odette and implores her forgiveness for his unwitting betrayal of her trust in him. They surrender to the joy of meeting but the enchanter appears and shatters their happiness; Siegfried must fulfil his oath and marry Odile, Odette, at the approach of dawn, must again become a swan. The lovers realize that it is better to die together while there is still time. The enchanter, alarmed, vanishes from sight. Siegfried and Odette cast themselves into the lake. The enchanter returns, but too late; their joint sacrifice has broken the spell and he falls dead.

Apotheosis. Through the waters of the lake, Odette and Siegfried voyage to the world of eternal happiness. Their journey is watched by the swan-maidens, now restored to their human form.

The village girls present garlands to Prince Siegfried (DAVID BLAIR)

The Pas de Six (MERIEL EVANS, MARY DRAGE, BRENDA TAYLOR)

Prince Siegfried drinks with his friend Benno and his Tutor, Wolfgang (ALEXIS RASSINE, LESLIE EDWARDS, RAY POWELL)

. . . and the Princ

Seeing a flock o
persuades the F
(DAVID BLAIR, 1

The Pas de Trois (ROSEMARY LINDSAY, PETER CLEGG, ANNETTE PAGE)

The Prince

The Pea

Cygnets (MARGARET MERCIER, JUDITH SINCLAIR, DOREEN WELLS, ANNETTE PAGE)

Two Swans (BRENDA TAYLOR, MARY DRAGE)

NADIA NERINA, ALEXIS RASSINE

SVETLANA BERIOSOVA, PHILIP CHATFIELD

*Prince Siegfried and the Princess Mother
enter the ballroom* (DAVID BLAIR, PAMELA MAY)

*Prince Siegfried and the Princess Mother
and the Master of Ceremonies*
(ALEXIS RASSINE, PAMELA MAY, LESLIE EDWARDS)

The Six Princesses

The Princess Mother asks the Prince to choose a bride . . .
. . . but none pleases him for his thoughts are of Odette, the Swan Princess

The Czardas (ANNETTE PAGE, PETER CLEGG)

The Czardas

The Spanish Dance

The Neapolitan Dance (JULIA FARRON, ALEXANDER GRANT)

149

The Mazurka

NADIA NERINA, ALEXIS RASSINE

Von Rothbart, the Wicked Magician,
and Odile, his daughter
(ARNOTT MADER, NADIA NERINA)

NADIA NERINA, ALEXIS RASSINE   153

The Princess Mother waits to receive Odile

Von Rothbart demands that Prince Siegfried shall swear he will love and marry Odile; but too late he finds it is all a trick
(NADIA NERINA, ALEXIS RASSINE)

(ELAINE FIFIELD, DAVID BLAIR)

Odile laughs as the court is thrown into confusion (BERYL GREY, ARNOTT MADER)

The Swans and Black Cygnets

Odette is distraught at her betrayal (NADIA NERINA)

Prince Siegfried implores forgiveness for his unwitting betrayal of her trust (NADIA NERINA, ALEXIS RASSINE)

157

(ELAINE FIFIELD, DAVID BLAIR)

SVETLANA BERIOSOVA, PHILIP CHATFIELD

MARGOT FONTEYN, MICHAEL SOMES

MARGOT FONTEYN

M